AFTERIMAGES

ZEN POEMS

AFTERIMAGES

. . .

ZEN POEMS

BY

SHINKICHI TAKAHASHI

. . .

Translated by Lucien Stryk and Takashi Ikemoto

ANCHOR BOOKS

Doubleday & Company, Inc.

Garden City, New York

Afterimages was originally published by The Swallow Press, Inc. The Anchor edition includes 14 poems which appeared in *Zen: Poems, Prayers, Sermons, Anecdotes, Interviews.*

SHINKICHI TAKAHASHI was born on Shikoku Island in 1901, and, in his teens, went to Tokyo to pursue a poetic career. He was the first Japanese to write dada poems, and is among the most prolific poets in modern Japan. From the start, he had a personal interest in Buddhism which, when he came into contact with the great Rinzai master Shizan Ashikaga, deepened into a lasting devotion to Zen. His full maturity in this discipline was finally testified to by Shizan. His later poetry is thoroughly inspired by the Zen spirit. He has also written many prose works, including several noteworthy expositions of Zen.

LUCIEN STRYK's most recent of five books of verse are *The Pit and Other Poems* and the forthcoming *Awakening*. His poems and essays have appeared in a number of anthologies and magazines, and he has received prizes for his verse and a grant, along with Takashi Ikemoto, from the National Translation Center to translate Zen poetry. He is the editor of *World of the Buddha*, the anthology *Heartland: Poets of the Midwest*, and (with Ikemoto) *Zen: Poems, Prayers, Sermons, Anecdotes, Interviews*. He has given poetry readings throughout the United States and England, and is presently teaching Oriental literature, poetry, and creative writing at Northern Illinois University.

TAKASHI IKEMOTO, born and educated in Japan, is Emeritus Professor of Yamaguchi University and Professor of English Literature at Otemon-Gakuin University in Ibaraki City. He is a Zen follower of longstanding, and a co-translator into Japanese of a volume of Thomas Merton's essays on Zen. His major concern for years has been the introduction of Japanese Zen to the West, and he has collaborated with Lucien Stryk in many Zen articles and *Zen: Poems, Prayers, Sermons, Anecdotes, Interviews*. He has contributed poetry and essays to numerous magazines in both Japan and the United States.

The translators join in dedicating this volume to
Tenzan Yasuda and Taigan Takayama
Zen masters of Yamaguchi

ACKNOWLEDGMENTS

The translators are indebted to the National Translation Center for grants which made possible the completion of this work, and to the Asian Literature Program of The Asia Society for its generous assistance. Some of the translations, and material incorporated in the Introductions, originally appeared in the following: Ann Arbor Review, BBC Third Programme, Carcanet, Chicago Review, Concerning Poetry, Jeopardy, Journals of Pierre Ménard, Literature East & West, London Magazine, Malahat Review, Michigan Quarterly Review, Modern Poetry in Translation, The Mountain Path, Orient/West, Poetry ('Canna,' 'Ice,' 'A Spray of Hot Air,' 'Sun Through the Leaves,' copyright 1970, Modern Poetry Association), Poetry Review, Prairie Schooner, Quixote, Road Apple Review, Southern Poetry Review, TriQuarterly, Twentieth Century, World of the Buddha (ed. by Lucien Stryk, Doubleday & Co., Inc., 1968), Yearbook of Comparative and General Literature, Zen: Poems, Prayers, Sermons, Anecdotes, Interviews (ed. by Lucien Stryk and Takashi Ikemoto, Doubleday & Co., Inc., 1965).

CONTENTS

FOREWORD

With Marxism on the wane, certain Japanese intellectuals seem recently to have begun reading musty old Buddhist sutras. This is not a tendency to be rejected wholesale; still, if they want to study Buddhism, they should do so thoroughly. They should not skim Buddhist literature and then talk about the Buddha's teaching knowingly. Theirs is but half-knowledge; they had better keep their lips closed. Nonetheless, they write about myokonin (Shin Sect devotees) or Kukai (founder of the Shingon Sect in Japan), and end in betraying their utter ignorance.

In Japan, since the decline of Buddhism, morals and manners have ceased to exist, and simultaneously respect for life and a view of social life such as the right relationship between young and old, have disappeared. To regain these is as difficult as to have the mini-skirt made long again.

What Shakyamuni aimed to do was to maintain both peace of the soul and peace of society, not with the aid of external things, but by simply sitting in Zen. He did Zen-sitting. This is the only historically established fact about him. Some Japanese intelligently refer to what Shakyamuni said on this occasion and on that. None of his sayings, however, have actually been transmitted; they must be taken with all reservation.

If we sit in Zen at all, we must model ourselves on Bodhidharma, who kept sitting till his buttocks grew rotten. We must have done with all words and letters, and attain Truth itself.

As a follower of the tradition of Zen which is above verbalization, I must confess that I feel ashamed of writing poems or having collections of them published in book form. Yet, since I believe in the Westernization of Buddhism, it is a pleasure to me that this collection of my poems has been published with the co-operation of Mr Takashi Ikemoto and Mr Lucien Stryk.

My wish is that, through this volume, the West will awake to the Buddha's Truth. It is my belief that Buddhism will travel round the world till it will bury its old bones in the ridge of the Himalayas.

SHINKICHI TAKAHASHI

Tokyo, Japan

INTRODUCTIONS

I

Shinkichi Takahashi is the only poet in Japan today who can properly be called a Zen poet. There are several poets who have some yearning after Zen or what savors of Zen; yet none of them has gained *satori*-experience, and from the Zen point of view a poet who is without this particular experience does not deserve to be called a Zen poet. In this sense, Takahashi, a genuine Zen-man, is unique in the history of modern Japanese poetry.

Takahashi was born in 1901 in a fishing village located in the middle of a long, narrow headland in western Shikoku, the smallest of the four main islands of Japan. 'I was born in the midst of the sea,' he has said, adding that his playmates in childhood were fish, which, as they were washed up on the beach by surf, he would catch in both hands. His daily life was bound with the sea, and sea-memories recur in his poetry's images.

Takahashi is largely a self-educated man, widely read in both secular and Buddhist literature. He left commercial high school just before graduation, and went to Tokyo seeking a literary career. Going down with typhus, and moneyless, Takahashi was sent to a charity hospital. He was forced to return to his village, where he happened to read newspaper articles on dadaism and, as he says, had his whole being galvanized. Back in Tokyo again, he worked as a waiter in a *shiruko-*

house (*shiruko* is red-bean soup with pieces of rice cake in it), and as a pantry boy in a newspaper office.

In 1921 he published a mimeographed collection of the poems he had written under the influence of dadaism; in the following year his dada manifesto and 'Three Dada Poems' were printed. In 1923 a collection of his poems entitled *Dadaist Shinkichi's Poetry* appeared, followed by *Gion Festival* (1924) and *Shinkichi Takahashi's Collected Poems* (1928). (None of Takahashi's books has been translated into English. I have translated the titles as a matter of convenience.) The first of these is one of the most significant and formative volumes in the history of modern Japanese poetry; it established the 22-year-old Takahashi as the foremost dadaist poet in Japan. A critic of the period called him a Japanese Rimbaud.

In 1928, at the suggestion of the late Shizan Ashikaga, an illustrious master of the Rinzai Zen sect, Takahashi went to Shogenji, a temple well known for the severity of discipline maintained there. He had read Marx and Lenin, and set out to discover whether Marxism or Zen had the ultimate truth. At Shogenji he participated in a one-week special retreat and applied himself strenuously to the training. One day, while walking along a corridor, he fell down unconscious; when he came to, he was off his head. Much later, he wrote that this incident was inevitable, considering how completely different the ascetic exercises were from his daily life and with what pure, youthful singlemindedness he had devoted himself to them. He was immediately sent back to his family home where he was locked in a two-mat room for three years. During this confinement, he wrote a large number of poems, versifying the ideas which possessed him. The fact that he ultimately survived this testing period is, in itself, remarkable, since mental disorders resulting from Zen discipline are usually difficult to cure.

Before the disastrous incident in the Shogenji temple and for years after, Takahashi was given to impulsive actions. More than once this brought him into trouble with the police, and it was in a police cell that he received a copy of his *Dadaist Shinkichi's Poetry*, which he is said to have torn up when it was handed to him through the bars.

Takahashi has lived chiefly by his writings. He visited Korea and China in 1939; in 1944 he entered a Tokyo newspaper office, and left it the following year after it had been bombed out. He married in 1951 at the age of 50, and is now leading with his family a Zennist-writer's life of serenity and activity which he would never have dreamed of in his turbulent youth.

Not long after his return to Tokyo in January, 1932, Takahashi began regularly to attend Master Shizan Ashikaga's lectures on Zen. Shizan, however, used to say: 'Attending Zen lectures cuts no ice. *Koan* exercise is all-important.' In 1935, therefore, Takahashi took up this Rinzai type of Zen study under Master Shizan. In the early years, after each one-week special Zen retreat, he would be exhausted, but he finally worked his way out and applied himself to the study of *koan* (Zen questions).

During almost 17 years of rigorous training under Shizan (though he also studied under a few other masters, for short periods), Takahashi experienced indescribable hardships but exultations of *satori*-enlightenment as well. He describes, in an essay, two of the *satori* experiences he had. He attained his first genuine enlightenment at the age of 40 during a special retreat in a mountain temple. It was his turn to enter the master's room to present his view of a *koan*, and as is prescribed, he struck a small hanging bell twice with a mallet to announce his entry. At the sound of the bell, he awakened to Selflessness. At that moment the sound was completely different from what he had heard so often. At last he grasped the root and essence of his being. The other *satori* he tells of came to him years later in a public bath. Coming out of the bathtub, he stooped down to grasp a washing-pail. At that instant something flashed across his mind; then he found that not a shadow of himself was to be seen. He opened his eyes wider and looked around, but there were no other bathers, no washing-pails, no steam, no voices. He saw once and for all that there existed nothing— no earth, no universe, no God, who, if ever he existed, was but a baby's stool floating on the hot water. He entered the bathtub again, and lay there comfortably, all limbs stretched out. This is a form of complete relaxation which one experiences at the moment of thorough *satori*, and which never leaves one throughout one's life.

By 1952, when he was 51 years old, Takahashi had learned all he could from Master Shizan, as is proved by the fact that the following year the master gave him, in his own calligraphy, 'The Moon-on-Water-Hall'. The words 'the moon-on-the-water-hall' come from the Zen phrase 'Seated in Zen in the moon-on-the-water-hall, / Conquer an army of devils in the mirror'. The 'moon-on-water' means Voidness, and 'mirror' means mind. Takahashi justly regards this calligraphy as a testimonial of his completion of the whole course of discipline under Shizan. He is one of the six or seven students who have been honored in such a way by the master. This particular kind of testimony is the highest honour to which a Zen disciple is entitled. Also, Takahashi records that once, during a special retreat, Shizan approved of his grasp of Zen. 'You're more than a match for me,' said the master. 'Go and take a rest.' From all this it is quite justifiable to call Takahashi a matured Zen-man; but matured humanly, let it be noted, because even Shakyamuni the Buddha and Bodhidharma, the first patriarch in China, are said to be still training themselves, and Takahashi humbly remarks that he has not yet completely entered the fortress of Zen. The sayings, writings, and doings of a matured Zennist are different from those of the undisciplined, and one cannot see into their real significance without having a proper sense of Zen.

Takahashi has published four books on Zen: *Stray Notes on Zen Study* (1958), *Mumonkan* (1958, an exposition of the famous collection of *koan* of the same title), *Rinzairoku* (1959, an exposition of the Chinese master Rinzai's words and deeds), and *A Life of Master Dogen* (1963). In *Stray Notes* he writes: '. . . since, to my thinking, God transcends existence, to conclude that there is no God is most relevant to him. As it is best not to think of such a God, praying to him is futile. Not only futile, but also immeasurably harmful; because man will make blunders, if, presupposing good and bad with his shallow wisdom, he clings to his hope of God's support.' A fundamental fact of Zen, as Takahashi grasped it, is that there is no self; without self, not a thing is; that is, not a thing is born. God, in the Zen, not Christian, sense is unborn, nor does he die.

Takahashi, as a poet and critic, records ideas and

images welling out of the depths of his *satori*-consciousness, and maintains that what is really fine necessarily embraces Zen. He is critical of all things that have no mature spirit of Zen in them. In his opinion, for example, neither the tea ceremony of Rikyu, the illustrious originator of the cult, nor the celebrated Noh drama is a substitute for Zen.

Following his mental recovery in 1932, Takahashi returned not only to Zen study but to his Tokyo literary career as well. The books of poetry he has produced since are: *Collected Witticisms* (1934), *Solar Eclipse* (1934), *A Selection of Shinkichi's Poems* (1936), *Rain Cloud* (1938), *Kirishima* (1942. Kirishima is the name of a mountain range of volcanoes in Southern Kyushu, half-way up one of which is located the ancient Kirishima Shrine.), *Father and Mother* (1943), *A Collection of Shinkichi Takahashi's Poems* (1949), *Shinkichi Takahashi's Collected Poems* (1952), *The Body* (1956), *Bream* (1962), and *Sparrow* (1966). Two anthologies include his pieces, both old and new: *Complete Works of Modern Poets*, vol. 5 (1960) and *Complete Works of Japanese Poets*, vol. 26 (1968).

The first collection of Takahashi's verses, *Dadaist Shinkichi's Poetry*, opens with a long prose-poem entitled 'Assertion Is Dadaist'. The poem begins,

> DADA asserts all, negates all;
> Infinity or Void: 'tobacco?' 'undershirt?' You
>   name it.

Takahashi goes on to declare: 'All that rises in the imagination is real; / The past is a fermented bean's future . . . / DADA finds ego in all, / Air vibration, bacilli's abhorrence . . .' He also refers to Buddhism, affirming: 'All is non-dual. From the Buddha's enlightenment learn: "All is all". I see all in all. Assertion is all.' Existence itself in terms of dada is dadaistic. Hence 'All things are interchangeable. Changeability is a value. Value is DADA'.

A way of thinking which is dominant in this dadaist piece remains characteristic of Takahashi's poetics; i.e., thinking in terms of assertion-negation, nothingness, non-duality, and interchangeability. But it must be noticed that the dada method, which for all the dadaist's affirmation to the contrary was relativistic, has been transmuted into Zen absolutism.

Following the publication in 1924 of his novel, *Dada*, Takahashi virtually abandoned dadaism as his central literary concern. He has written several articles on this movement. In his earlier reminiscences he was prone to denounce dada, saying that it was rather shallow, something like a bubble, that it contained only a modicum of 'fox-Zen', that is, fake Zen. He argued: 'If there is any legacy at all of dada and surrealism, it is simply that they have helped accelerate the desolation and downfall of the Occident, and prompt the ascendancy of the self-awakened Asians.' On the other hand, he refuted those who would discover nothing in the declaration of Zaller, a protagonist of dada, but a form of pessimism and nihilism; he argued that *Dada* had spread widely and rapidly because it had an undercurrent of cogent philosophy which would stir people out of the spiritual devastation of World War I. Later, he wrote in further defence: 'There is in dada something positive that affirms all from where all has been negated and demolished.' This constructive revaluation of dadaism is no doubt largely due to Takahashi's maturity in Zen, which goes beyond mere negation and leads to affirmation, in the truly absolute sense of the word.

Takahashi's view of the word is in complete accord with Zen. Zen rejects words and letters as mere pointers to the moon, i.e., Suchness. Rejection of language demands desperate efforts from the student; he must die to the concept-bound self in order to be resurrected to Suchness. That is why Takahashi maintains: 'In short, confidence and action is all. One would present a sorry sight if one kept loitering, fascinated, within the fold of literature. True poetry is born out of the very despair that the word is useless and poetry is to be abandoned.' Holding as he does such a severe view of poetry, it is not surprising to hear him say that none of the pieces of the greatest Zen *haiku* poet, Basho, has ever moved him deeply.

Takahashi's distrust of the word is seen in his poem, 'Words'. He has written several other verses on the same subject. In one of them he says:

> Put things in trimmest order by the word
> And it's still a mere matter of words:
> Nothing settled or changed.

Another verse reads, in part:

> The word, with its void and crevices,
> Has no real being.
> What's grasped by words is vulnerable;
> Richer, more poetic the flux of realities.

Zen is a religion of word-denunciation, but of all the Buddhist sects, Zen has the greatest volume of literature, and this is true particularly of poetic productions. Maintaining that poetry and Zen are of a kind, almost all noted Zen priests wrote in rhyme, and a good num-

8

ber of them have left copious works in verse—a phenomenon to be seen in none of the other Buddhist sects. The fact is that Zen rejects words and letters simply because all of us adhere to them in disregard of the naked truth. But fundamentally, as Bodhidharma or some later Zen scholar declared, words and letters can embody Buddhism in themselves. It is in this conviction that Zen priests have engaged in literary activities.

Takahashi, who has followed the Zen tradition in all its phases, is fully aware of the value of the word. True, he says he demolishes words for the sake of the Fact of Zen, but as a poet he has no means to demonstrate the indescribability of the final Fact except by resorting to words. To this end, he handles words no less discreetly than the literary Zen masters of the past. Takahashi does not end by merely negating the value of verbal expression; ultimately, even while negating, he is affirming. He writes in the lines quoted above: 'It's still a mere matter of words: / Nothing settled or changed', but seen from the Zen position, everything is settled by the word as un-settled. This is a fact which reveals itself to the inner eye of an experienced Zennist, and no doubt it was this final reality that Takahashi had in mind when he wrote the lines.

For all his destructive criticism of verbalization, there are found in Takahashi's writings affirmative and appreciative remarks about the word. He says that he has not ignored the beauty of language, which is apparent in the subtle beauty of his poems and his scrupulous attention to poetic form. Furthermore, he writes in one of his essays: 'Words have infinite meaning.' This is a remark no mere word-demolisher would ever make. The significance of Takahashi's matured Zen consciousness in relation to poetic expression is illustrated by his recent commentary on the following two quotations.

> I was neither born
> Nor have licked the sun.

> Because nothing exists,
> I am neither born
> Nor die.

Of these, the first is from 'The Deaf', one of his 'Three Dada Poems' published in 1922 (the words quoted are spoken by an earthworm), and the second is from one of his recent pieces. Takahashi says that there is a difference between the two monosyllables, 'was' and 'am' and that between these two little words lies a distance of almost a half century. It was his matured Zen experience that enabled him to write 'am neither born' instead of 'was neither born' in representing the truth of birthlessness, one of the most important teachings of Zen.

Takahashi was and is a unique poet; still, he neither gained a wide popularity as a dadaist poet nor has he received the recognition he deserves as a Zen poet. This is not surprising, considering that dadaism in Japan was only known among a small group of intellectuals and that both poets and readers are ill-informed of the Zen discipline Takahashi has undergone. In general, readers have an inadequate knowledge of Zen, and Zen followers are mostly indifferent to modern, free verse forms, concerning themselves primarily with classical Chinese poetry or Japanese *waka* and *haiku*. The result is that only a limited number of poets possessed of some sense of Zen are in a position properly to appreciate Takahashi's poetry as Zen poetry. Takahashi himself says: 'Those who understand my poetry have always been very few in number. Indeed, there may be none understands it.' Takahashi seems to set no great value on the appraisal or appreciation of his verse, even by those poets who are sympathetic toward Zen. It is true that they write with eloquence about him, and yet it is questionable how deeply they have penetrated the mind of this Zen poet.

Critics agree that it is in *The Body* (1956) that a world of rare beauty is created in which Buddhist thought and poetic imagery are perfectly harmonized with one another. One critic says that this work is among the greatest literary monuments that post-War Japan has produced. Another writes that Takahashi, crossing the valley of remorse and tears, has entered the land of eternal serenity, where he, a man of perfect freedom, gives free play not to force but to airy wisdom, and that anarchical though what he depicts may appear, it is in heavenly order because of his self-abnegation. One contemporary poet says of Takahashi's diction that the dada style of declaration wedded with Zen has given a vigorous, rectilinear sonority to his phrasing, adding to its stratified depth. Still another poet, detecting in Takahashi a free and easy cosmic sense, states: 'Takahashi's poetry is piquancy itself, just as Zen, the quintessence of Buddhism, bawls out by means of its concise vocabulary a sort of piquant ontology. . . . Where does this enlivened feature come from? It comes from his strange disposition which enables him to sense the homogeneity of all things including human beings. It is further due to his own method of versification: he clashes his idea of timelessness against the temporality of all phenomena to cause a fissure, through which he lets us see personally and convincingly the reality of limitless space.' This seems a perceptive analysis of Takahashi's poetry, however dualistic the point of view. Still, the remark about Takahashi's versification is misleading; it gives one the impression that his poetry furnishes the reader with a fragmentary view of the Void. Rather it is that each of his poems, because he is identified with the Void at any moment, is in itself a full unveiling of the Void in its totality. An old Zen saying goes: 'In life is realized the whole phase of life; in death the whole phase of death.' This is to say that in everything is realized the whole of the Void, the final Fact, nothing lacking, nothing in excess. Takahashi writes in this all-comprehensive state of mind, though it is always backed by absolute negation.

Critics of Takahashi are prone to refer to surrealistic imagery in his verse, but the term 'surrealistic' calls for a few words of caution. 'Surrealistic' in relation to poetic imagery is suggestive of verbal play aiming at a conjunction of the unexpected and heterogeneous. In comparison, imagery in Zen verse is an immediate expression of the ultimate Fact inasmuch as a Zennist's whole personality is projected into it. (One may object, saying that this remark about a Zen poet applies equally to a non-Zen poet, but the latter cannot be said to have arrived at the ultimate Fact as exacted by Zen, hence his complacency or restlessness.) For example, Takahashi's images in the lines 'Suddenly your face / Is large as the universe' ('Snow Wind') or 'The sun roams the bottom of the sea' ('Penguins') represent a Zen fact which is in itself the final Fact. Your face, in the non-dualistic world of Zen, can grow as large as the universe or, conversely, as small as an atom. Because there is nothing, anything can happen. Here it is to be recalled that there are applied *koan* in the *koan* system of the Rinzai branch of the Japanese Zen sect such as 'Go bind Mt. Fuji with a rush and bring it here' or 'Pass in and out of this tobacco pipe'. To make use of Takahashi's imagery, the Zen student may be demanded to show his face as large as the universe, and so on. The objective of applied *koan* is to train the student so that he can be his own master in this world of intricate differentiation. In poetry, of course, imagery must be relevant to the content of a piece; it is certainly not that Takahashi, as a Zen poet, is free to introduce any kind of imagery without detriment to his poems. I am fully conscious of the importance of this problem in poetics, and fear that I have laid undue emphasis on the Zen aspect of imagery in Takahashi's verse. Still, I have done so for two reasons: one is that without a proper understanding of the absolute freedom which makes a Zen-man what he is, the reader may be tempted to consider some of Takahashi's images weird or even absurd; the other is that, as he states in his Foreword, Takahashi desires the reader to 'awake to the Buddha's Truth' through this volume; which is to say that he wants his poetry to be read not simply as secular verse but as religious poetry, i.e., Zen poetry.

All but one of the 91 poems in this volume have been chosen from 7 of Takahashi's later works: 15 from *A Collection of Shinkichi Takahashi's Poems*, 12 from *Shinkichi Takahashi's Collected Poems*, 27 from *The Body*, 8 from *Complete Works of Modern Poets*, 13 from *Bream*, and 15 from *Sparrow*. (The exception, 'Horse', was drawn from a magazine.) Takahashi has written in all much more than one thousand pieces; 91 is, therefore, a moderate number, and yet this selection, we believe, well represents him.

The arrangement of the pieces is not chronological, nor does it follow any other external principle; but in order to make for a sort of organic whole, the content of each poem has been taken into consideration. The title of the book from which each piece has been taken is given in the Contents. The abbreviations of the titles used are as follows: CTSP for *A Collection of Shinkichi Takahashi's Poems*; TSCP for *Shinkichi Takahashi's Collected Poems*; Body for *The Body*; and CWMP for *Complete Works of Modern Poets*.

What we aimed at in our necessarily free translation was to preserve the Zen spirit of the original poems. Our translations can be divided into four classes: (*a*) Those following the originals as closely as possible; these constitute by far the greatest part of the work. (*b*) Those with several or more lines omitted; conspicuous examples are 'Rat on Mount Ishizuchi', 'Red Waves', 'What Is Moving', 'One Hundred Billionth of a Second', 'Sun', 'Magpie', and 'White Paper'. (*c*) Those giving the gist of originals: 'Spring Snow', 'Immutability', and the second of the poems entitled 'Time'. (*d*) The one in which only a part of the original is given: 'Man'.

Widespread and increasingly serious interest in Zen is evident more in the United States than in Japan. With Takahashi, I hope that this book will contribute toward a better recognition in the West of the value of Zen in a time when all the people in the world are being consciously or unconsciously diseased by self-alienation under the pressure of advanced technology. Zen is the one thing that makes it possible to overcome this disease of self-alienation; through it man realizes Selflessness in the Absolute Void and is reborn to supermundane freedom. Takahashi's Zen poetry is an exteriorization of this ineffable Selflessness and freedom.

I cannot conclude this note without expressing our deep gratitude to Takahashi for the unfailing cooperation he lent to our project; he enlightened us on difficult lines in some of his poems and furnished us with precious biographical information.

TAKASHI IKEMOTO

Yamaguchi, Japan

1

Like that of most important poets, East or West, Shin-kichi Takahashi's work can be read on a number of levels, each rewarding, yet the reader should bear in mind as he moves through *Afterimages* that the poems are those of a Zen Buddhist.

Since the Kamakura period (13th century) many of Japan's finest writers have been, if not actually involved in its study and practice, at least attracted by Zen Buddhism, which some would claim has been among the most seminal philosophies, in its effect on the arts, that the world has known. To take a contemporary example, Yasunari Kawabata, Nobel Laureate and author of among other important works the novel *Yukiguni* (*Snow Country*), is as a writer of fiction greatly indebted to the haiku aesthetic, in which Zen principles dominate. Another, Yukio Mishima, writes plays based on the Noh drama form, which like the art of the haiku is closely associated with Zen. Such writers have been directly or indirectly affected by Zen, which, as Arthur Waley has pointed out, has always been the philosophy of artists, its language that in which poetry and painting have always been discussed. Unlike Takahashi, however, very few contemporary Japanese writers have trained under a Zen master. He is widely recognized as the foremost living Zen poet.

The poet's work is best read, then, in a rather special context, its chief (perhaps most obvious) quality being what Zennists call *zenki*, spontaneous activity free of forms, flowing from the formless self, leading to the bold thrust of his metaphor. No less important, and clearly Buddhist, is his awareness of pain, human and animal, though it should be evident in this day and age that his frequent references to things 'atomic' need not be seen as exclusively Buddhist or Japanese. That many of his poems are 'irrational' cannot be denied, but if once irrationality was a suspect element in Western poetry (it has never been in Oriental), it is less so today—witness the popularity of artists who, like Takahashi, employ the surrealist method if only in modified form. Zen and Taoist poets have always been unconventional in their methods and attitudes, and Takahashi's poems sin no more against rationality than Hakuin's, the greatest figure in Japanese Rinzai Zen. Here is a typical piece by the 18th-century master:

> You no sooner attain the great void
> Than body and mind are lost together.
> Heaven and Hell—a straw.
> The Buddha-realm, Pandemonium—shambles.
> Listen: a nightingale strains her voice,
>   serenading the snow.
> Look: a tortoise wearing a sword climbs
>   the lampstand.
> Should you desire the great tranquility,
> Prepare to sweat white beads.

In his introduction to our 1965 volume *Zen: Poems, Prayers, Sermons, Anecdotes, Interviews*, Takashi Ikemoto writes, 'To a Zen poet, a thing of beauty or anything in nature *is* the Absolute. Hence his freedom from rationality and his recourse to uncommon symbols. Yet ultimately what he portrays is concrete, not a dreamy fancy or vision.' Surely one of the strengths of Takahashi's poetry is its concreteness—a particular animal or flower, a precisely rendered (however unusual) state of mind. And yet much of the poetry is admittedly very difficult, one reason being that as in the case of all Zen poets, many of Takahashi's poems read like *koans*, or Zen problems for meditation, the purpose of which is to make clear to the seeker of answers that there is no distinction between subject and object, the search and the thing sought are one and the same. One awakening to such an identification attains the state of *muga*, an important step toward the goal of Zen training, *satori* (enlightenment). One of the best-known koans is Hakuin's 'What is the sound of one hand clapping?'

If read with some understanding of the philosophy, Zen poetry need not be obscure. To give an idea of how a trained Zennist reads it, here is Takahashi's 'The Peach' followed by an analysis of the poem by Taigan Takayana, a master of Yamaguchi (the quotation is from one of the interviews in the same volume):

A little girl under a peach tree,
Whose blossoms fall into the entrails
Of the earth.

There you stand, but a mountain may be there
Instead; it is not unlikely that the earth
May be yourself.

You step against a plate of iron and half
Your face is turned to iron. I will smash
Flesh and bone

And suck the cracked peach. She went up the
  mountain
To hide her breasts in the snowy ravine.
Women's legs

Are more or less alike. The leaves of the peach
  tree
Stretch across the sea to the end of
The continent.

The sea was at the little girl's beck and call.
I will cross the sea like a hairy
Caterpillar

And catch the odour of your body.

Taigan Takayama's comment: Most interesting, from
both the Zen and the literary points of view. Let's be-
gin with the former: an Avatamsaka doctrine holds
that the universe can be observed from the four angles
of (1) phenomena, (2) noumenon, (3) the identity of
noumenon and phenomena, and (4) the mutual iden-
tity of phenomena. Now, whether he was aware of it or
not, the poet depicted a world in which noumenon and
phenomena are identical. Considering the poem with
Zen in mind, the lesson to be drawn, I suppose, is that
one should not loiter on the way but proceed straight
to one's destination—the viewpoint of the mutual iden-
tity of phenomena. But from a literary point of view,
the significance and the charm of the poem lies in its
metaphorical presentation of a world in which noume-
non and phenomena are identified with each other.

More generally—and to return to Takashi Ikemoto's
description of Zen poetry—a few more features of the
poetry may be cited. There are 'conciseness, rigour,
volitionality, virility, and serenity.' Yet, in spite of the
importance, considering the poet's intention, of analys-
ing the Zen elements in Takahashi's poems, they should
be fairly intelligible to those familiar with much mod-
ern poetry, even in English translation (if not, the poet
is less to blame than his translators), for as has often

been said that which is most translatable in poetry is the image, and it is in his use of imagery that, from a purely technical view, Takahashi is perhaps most unique:

> My legs lose themselves
> Where the river mirrors daffodils
> Like faces in a dream.
>> —A Wood in Sound

> The peak of Mount Ishizuchi
> Has straightened the spine
> Of the Island of Futana.
>> —Rat on Mount Ishizuchi

> Sunbeams, spokes of a stopped wheel,
> Blaze through the leaves of a branch.
>> —Sun Through the Leaves

Though as a free-verse poet Takahashi has not cultivated the telling economy of the haiku and waka writers, a number of his pieces are as spare and sharp as the best haiku. 'Words' is a good example:

> I don't take your words
> Merely as words.
> Far from it.

> I listen
> To what makes you talk—
> Whatever that is—
> And me listen.

Yet Takahashi wishes to be judged—if judged as poet at all—as one whose work expresses more than anything else the Zen spirit. A poem like 'Canna', which in addition to being effective poetry communicates strongly one of the Bodhisattva ideals of Mahayana Buddhism, self-sacrifice for others, is therefore of particular importance. Here are the last stanzas:

> She often talks of suicide.
> Scared, I avoid her cold face.
>
> Again today she spoke
> Of certain premonitions.
> How can I possibly
> Save this woman's life?
>
> Living as if dead, I shall
> Give up my own. She must live.

A number of the poet's pieces clearly concern Zen discipline, 'Life Infinite' being typical:

> Beyond words, this no-thingness within,
> Which I've become. So to remain
>
> Only one thing's needed: Zen sitting.
> I think, breathe with my whole body—
>
> Marvellous. The joy's so pure,
> It's beyond love making, anything.
>
> I can see, live anywhere, everywhere.
> I need nothing, not even life.

In spite of its apparent simplicity, such a poem is very difficult to understand outside a Zen context (and extremely hard to render properly in another language). Take the last line: if it had been given somewhat less

21

paradoxically as, say, 'I need nothing, fearing not even death', the poet would have been misrepresented and the reader misled, for there is no 'fear' of death possible in Zen. While poems such as 'Life Infinite' may not be quite as rewarding poetically as most of Takahashi's pieces, they are understandably of considerable importance to him and thus must not be bypassed by one interested in him as a Zen poet.

While the alert reader may find it possible to read a poem like 'Life Infinite' with little difficulty, there is another kind of poem which though dealing as directly with the Zen experience could prove puzzling. 'Destruction', which exhibits as well as any the quality of *zenki* defined above, is such a piece:

The universe is forever falling apart—
No need to push the button,
It collapses at a finger's touch:
Why, it barely hangs on the tail of a sparrow's eye.

The universe is so much eye secretion,
Hordes leap from the tips
Of your nostril hairs. Lift your right hand:
It's in your palm. There's room enough
On the sparrow's eyelash for the whole.

A paltry thing, the universe:
Here is all strength, here the greatest strength.
You and the sparrow are one
And, should he wish, he can crush you.
The universe trembles before him.

In this poem there is not only a 'spontaneous activity free of forms, flowing from the formless self', but the destruction of the most rigid form of all—a conceptual universe. What the poet seems to be saying is that man, unlike the sparrow, has created forms which confine and frustrate him, and that until he sees that they have no reality, are paltry, 'so much eye secretion', he will continue to tremble before them, their prisoner. He must, in other words, live as freely as the sparrow who, should he wish, can by crushing the universe crush its creator. Indeed all forms, not the universe alone, 'tremble before him'.

Throughout Takahashi's work, as in all Zen writing, such attitudes are prominent, yet they need not be seen as peculiarly Zennist or, for that matter, Oriental. In his 'Worpswede' the German poet Rainer Maria Rilke writes what could very well serve as a paraphrase of a poem like 'Destruction':

> We play with obscure forces, which we cannot lay hold of, by the names we give them, as children play with fire, and it seems for a moment as if all the energy had lain unused in things until we came to apply it to our transitory life and its needs. But repeatedly . . . these forces shake off their names and rise . . . against their little lords, no, not even *against*—they simply rise, and civilizations fall from the shoulders of the earth. . . .

2

Shinkichi Takahashi might have written, as Chekhov wrote to a friend, 'A conscious life without a definite philosophy is no life, rather a burden and a nightmare'. That the poet has found such a definite philosophy in

23

Zen Buddhism has hopefully been demonstrated, and it is doubtlessly true that his work is distinguished largely because of the philosophy underlying it. He has worked hard, as all Zennists must, to discover those truths which can hardly be expressed in anything less than poetry. Hence if the Western reader interested in Zen wants some indication of what the philosophy can mean to a practitioner, he should seek it in the arts associated with the philosophy, particularly the poetry. With that in mind it might be useful to give some idea of the manner in which Zen masters of the past employed poetry to express insights afforded by their philosophy.

Even in translation, or such at least is the hope, Zen poetry is so suggestive in itself that, as in the case of a piece like 'Life Infinite', explication is rarely necessary. Older Japanese Zennists did not theorize about the poems they would write from time to time, and for good reason: to them poetry was not, as so often in the West, an art to be cultivated but a means by which an attempt at the nearly inexpressible might be made. Though some of their poems are called 'satori' poems, others 'death' poems, and some are little more than interpretations, meant for presentation to a master, of koans, all the poems deal with spiritually momentous experiences. There are, in other words, no 'finger exercises', and though some Zen poems are comparatively light there is not one that is less than fully inspired. Indeed, when one considers the Zennist's traditional goal, the all-or-nothing striving after illumination, this is hardly to be wondered at.

Poets of the Chinese Ch'an sect ('Zen' is the Japanese transliteration of 'Ch'an'), on whose works the early Zennists modeled their own, were less reluctant to theorize. They speak of the need, for example, to attain a state of calm, making it possible for the poet to get the spirit of nature into his poems. If the Zen masters considered it improper to write on the nature of poetry, many affected by Zen did not, and great haiku poets like Basho had disciples who would transcribe their words. Here is Basho's disciple Doho:

> The Master said: 'Learn about a pine tree from a pine tree, and about a bamboo plant from a bamboo plant.' He meant that the poet should detach the mind from himself, and by 'learn' that he should enter into the object, the whole of its delicate life, feeling as it feels. The poem follows of itself.

Another way of thinking about this most important principle of Zen aesthetics, and a convenient one for Westerners, is to recall Keats's 'Negative Capability', by which the poet meant to suggest that the true artist does not assert his own personality, even if he imagines himself possessed of one. Rather he identifies as far as possible with the object of his contemplation, its personality, without feeling that he has to *understand* it. There are many old Zen poems about this state of mind, one of the best being Bunan's:

> The moon's the same old moon,
> The flowers exactly as they were,
> Yet I've become the thingness
> Of all the things I see!

Zen poetry has always been highly symbolic, and the moon, as in Bunan's poem, is a common symbol. It should be remembered, in relation to the use of such symbols, that as religion Zen is a Mahayana sect, and that the Zennist searches, always within, for the indivisible moon reflected not only on the sea but on each dewdrop. To discover this, the *Dharmakaya*, in all things, whether while sitting in meditation or writing a poem, is to discover one's own Buddha-nature. Most Zen poems delineate graphically what the spiritual eye has been awakened to, a view of things seen as for the first time, in their eternal aspect. Here is a 13th century poem by the master Daito:

> At last I've broken Unmon's barrier!
> There's exit everywhere—east, west; north, south.
> In at morning, out at evening; neither host nor
>   guest.
> My every step stirs up a little breeze.

And here is Shinkichi Takahashi's 'Cock':

> Getting soaked on rainy days,
> Tramping snow on snowy,
> Riding wind on windy days,
> Strutting on the fine—
> I'll crow a lifetime through.

One of the most important Zen principles, and it is one that seems to appeal for obvious reasons to Westerners interested in the philosophy, is the need to 'let go'. It is a principle based on the idea, demonstrably true, that one never gets what is grasped for. Seek not, in other words, and ye shall find. Here is how the 19th-century master Kanemitsu-Kogun expresses it:

My hands released at last, the cliff soars
Ten thousand meters, the plowshare sparks,
All's consumed with my body. Born again,
The lanes run straight, the rice well in the ear.

Traditionally death poems are written or dictated by masters just before dying. The master looks back upon his life and, in a few highly compressed lines, expresses for the benefit of his disciples his state of mind at the inevitable hour. The Void, the great Penetralium of Zen, is often mentioned in the death poems. The mind, it is thought, is a void or empty space in which objects are stripped of their objectivity and reduced to their essence. The following death poem by the 14th-century master Fumon is typical:

Magnificent! Magnificent!
No-one knows the final word.
The ocean bed's aflame,
Out of the void leap wooden lambs.

It would be misleading to claim that only Zennists exhibit such stoicism before death. In his brilliant essay 'Artists and Old Age' Gottfried Benn tells of the diamond dealer Solomon Rossbach who, just before leaping from the top of the Empire State Building, scrawled what is by any standards a great death poem:

No more above,
No more below—
So I leap off.

Because of the extremely private nature of *dokusan*,

or the meeting of master and disciple, during which the latter is expected to offer interpretations of the koan, often in the form of poetry, not too much can be said about those Zen poems based on koans. Perhaps the following anecdote will give some idea of what takes place at such an interview, particularly the manner in which the disciple's poem is handled.

Kanzan (1277–1360), the National Teacher, gave Fujiwara-Fujifusa the koan 'Original Perfection'. For many days Fujifusa sat in Zen. When he finally had an intuition, he composed the following:

> Once possessed of the mind that has always been,
> Forever I'll benefit men and devas both.
> The benignity of the Buddha and Patriarchs can hardly be repaid.
> Why should I be reborn as horse or donkey?

When he called on Kanzan with the poem, this dialogue took place:

Kanzan: Where's the mind?
Fujifusa: It fills the great void.
Kanzan: With what will you benefit men and devas?
Fujifusa: I shall saunter along the stream, or sit down to watch the gathering clouds.
Kanzan: Just how do you intend repaying the Buddha and Patriarchs?
Fujifusa: The sky's over my head, the earth under my feet.
Kanzan: All right, but why shouldn't you be reborn as horse or donkey?

At this Fujifusa got to his feet and bowed.

'Good!' Kanzan said with a loud laugh. 'You've gained
    perfect satori.'

Though satori, death and koan interpretation figure
heavily in old Zen poetry, many of the poems deal with
nature and man's place in it. The Buddha-nature is
by no means man's alone, being discoverable in all that
exists, animate or inanimate. As Arthur Waley puts it
in his *Zen Buddhism and Its Relation to Art:*

> Stone, river and tree are alike parts of the great
> hidden Unity. Thus man, through his Buddha-
> nature or universalized consciousness, possesses an
> intimate means of contact with nature. The song
> of birds, the noise of waterfalls, the rolling of
> thunder, the whispering of wind in the pine trees
> —all these are utterances of the Absolute.

And as Shinkichi Takahashi expresses it in 'Wind
Among the Pines':

> The wind blows hard among the pines
> Toward the beginning
> Of an endless past.
> Listen: you've heard everything.

3

It should be clear from the foregoing that Shinkichi
Takahashi is an important Zen poet, but what is it,
apart from his philosophy, that makes him a fine con-
temporary poet, read with almost as much apprecia-
tion in Chicago, say, as in Tokyo? There are many rea-
sons for the appeal of his work, but surely the chief is

the breathtaking freedom of his imagination, best seen perhaps in his empathy with the life of creatures. For in order to empathize fully, one must imagine fully, enter the world of one's subject spontaneously, without holding back. In poem after poem Takahashi reveals how totally he is able to identify with his subject. Here is the first stanza of 'Sparrow in Winter':

Breastdown fluttering in the breeze,
The sparrow's full of air holes.
Let the winds of winter blow,
Let them crack a wing, two,
The sparrow doesn't care.

And here the first two stanzas of 'Crow':

The crow, spreading wide wings,
Flapped lazily off.
Soon her young will be doing the same,
Firm wings rustling.

It's hard to tell the male
Crow from the female,
But their love, their mating
Must be fresh as their flight.

In such work, so scornful of logical development, the poet achieves something close to pure poetry, which can come only of an unfettered imagination. Now pure poetry is as difficult to define as to write, yet an attempt must be made: if we take into account those elements of poetry which, as far back as Aristotle, have been considered pre-eminent, chiefly metaphor and verbal energy, then we are forced to conclude that pure poetry is very rare indeed and that much that goes by the name of poetry is really little more than metered prose. In modern criticism a great deal of space is devoted to the analysis of technical experimentation, those ingenuities which so often cloak hollowness. Yet the serious poetry-reading public is not easily fooled, and a poet like Dylan Thomas can capture it readily enough because his work is comparatively pure, charged with vital metaphor.

The fine poet is always something of an anomaly, and can be likened to a perfectly functioning sensorium, one sense related organically to all others—the eye to the ear, and so on. Whether such a man turns to poetry because it is as natural for him to do so as the bird to sing, or because the writing of poems may confer a distinction not attainable otherwise, no one can say. Nor can one tell whether the themes associated with serious poetry—social justice, for example—come naturally to such a poet or are just there as suitable subjects to engage the imagination of the gifted human. When we hear a poet like Takahashi claiming that his philosophy is more important to him than anything he writes, we are perhaps entitled to a certain degree of scepticism, yet we must bear in mind that traditionally Zen is not only the philosophy of artists, it is essentially, in its highest forms, elitist. The Sixth Patriarch of Zen, the Chinese Hui-Neng (683–762), who was handed 'the robe and the law' of succession solely because of the insight expressed in a short poem written for his master, claims in his *Platform Scripture:*

> . . . there is no distinction between sudden enlightenment and gradual enlightenment in the Law, except that some people are intelligent and

others stupid. Those who are ignorant realize the truth gradually, while the enlightened ones attain it suddenly.

Just as the gifted man finds it possible to attain his ends more quickly in a philosophy like Zen, he can, once he sets his mind to it, attain in the arts what others, however sincere and assiduous, cannot hope to reach. The fact is—and were it acknowledged—that most writing on art deals with the phenomenology of failure, with why X were he more like Z might turn out to be slightly superior to Y. We wind up distrusting much criticism, and aesthetic theorizing, because we find that in spite of it, and all the standards and criteria it propounds as essential to the judgment of art, a work either engages the imagination, or it doesn't. Which is why Ezra Pound could claim that 'It is better to present one Image in a lifetime than to produce voluminous works'.

Though as a Zennist Takahashi disclaims any ambition as an artist, he must—as must all poets, whether working within a particular discipline or not—be judged first of all as an artist. In order for a poet, Oriental or Western, to become an artist, he must become a maker of the new, and that which chiefly distinguishes the poem of an artist from that of a writer of verse is that it can stand alone, palpable as a chair, unsupported by anything outside itself and indifferent to the uses made of it. The work of art is not a vehicle of preachment or propaganda, and whatever the idea in the name of which it was brought into being—Zen, Marxism, Art itself—it stands or falls on the degree to which it possesses those qualities which, though seemingly peculiar to its medium, are rightly seen as held in common by all real works of art—appropriate form, freshness of detail, integrality of tone and relevance to human experience. It is in the belief that in addition to being a true Zennist Shinkichi Takahashi is an important artist that Takashi Ikemoto and I offer the experience of his poems to English-speaking readers.

LUCIEN STRYK

DeKalb, Illinois, U.S.A.

The following is a reproduction of Shinkichi Takahashi's own calligraphy for the title poem, 'Afterimages', which appears in translation on page 137

残像　　　　高橋新吉

阿蘇の噴煙が
海をへだてた岸辺に降ってきた
火山灰が畑の桑の葉にも
雀の頭にも白くついた
熔岩の鰐は口を開いたままである
雀は化石の中の枝にとまっている
月が眉の下に照っていた

朽木にへばりつった水大蜥蜴

震動する三崎の尾

頭の中に雲がたよっている

その雲は実に美しい

夜が目を開くと

物は消えて遠くなっている

眞はアキメクラ

いつでもバラ色の空間を見ている

その木に赤い花が咲いていたとはいうな

彼女の鼻歌だけがつづいて

こちらに迫ってきた

一切は残像に過ぎない

足の裏に水が流れている

その水は実に冷い

竪穴の甕棺に埋められた者は
噴火口を半眼にして　翼で
地球の燃え尽きる火柱をかき立てる

AFTERIMAGES

ZEN POEMS

A WOOD IN SOUND

The pinetree sways in the smoke,
Which streams up and up.
There's a wood in sound.

My legs lose themselves
Where the river mirrors daffodils
Like faces in a dream.

A cold wind and the white memory
Of a sasanqua.
Warm rain comes and goes.

I'll wait calmly on the bank
Till the water clears
And willows start to bud.

Time is singed on the debris
Of air raids.
Somehow, here and now, I am another.

ACHING OF LIFE

There must be something better,
But I'm satisfied just as I am.

Monkeys sport deep in the forest,
Fish shoot up the mountain stream.

If there's change, there's also repose—
Which soon must suffer change.

Along the solar orbit of the night,
I feel life's constant aching:

Smack in the middle of the day,
I found moonlight between a woman's legs.

SNOW WIND

There's nothing more to see:
Snow in the nandin's leaves
And, under it, the red-eyed
Rabbit lies frozen.

I'll place everything on
Your eyeballs, the universe.
There's nothing more to see:
Nandin berries are red, snow white.

The rabbit hopped twice in the cool
Breeze and everyone disappeared,
Leaving the barest scent.
The horizon curves endlessly

And now there's no more light
Around the rabbit's body.
Suddenly your face
Is large as the universe.

CANNA

A red canna blooms,
While between us flickers
A death's head, dancing there
Like a pigmy or tiny ball.

We try to catch it—
Now it brushes my hands,
Now dallies with her feet.

She often talks of suicide.
Scared, I avoid her cold face.

Again today she spoke
Of certain premonitions.
How can I possibly
Save this woman's life?

Living as if dead, I shall
Give up my own. She must live.

TIME

Time like a lake breeze
Touched his face,
All thought left his mind.

One morning the sun, menacing,
Rose from behind a mountain,
Singeing—like hope—the trees.

Fully awakened, he lit his pipe
And assumed the sun-inhaling pose:
Time poured down—like rain, like fruit.

He glanced back and saw a ship
Moving towards the past. In one hand
He gripped the sail of eternity,

And stuffed the universe into his eyes.

THE PINK SUN

White petals on the black earth,
Their scent filling her nostrils.

Breathe out and all things swell—
Breathe in, they shrink.

Let's suppose she suddenly has four legs—
That's far from fantastic.

I'll weld ox hoofs onto her feet—
Sparks of the camellia's sharp red.

Wagging her pretty little tail,
She's absorbed in kitchenwork.

Look, she who just last night
Was a crone is girl again,

An alpine rose blooming on her arm.
High on a Himalayan ridge

The great King of Bhutan
Snores in the pinkest sun.

THISTLES

Thistles bloomed in the vast moonlit
Cup of the Mexican sands.

Thistles bloomed on the round hillock
Of a woman's heart.

The stained sea was choked with thistles,
Sky stowed away in thistle stalks.

Thistles, resembling a male corpse, bloomed
Like murex from a woman's side.

At the thorny root of a yellow cactus plant
A plucked pigeon crouched,

And off in the distance a dog whimpered,
As if swallowing hot air.

RAT ON MOUNT ISHIZUCHI

Snow glitters on the divine rocks
At the foot of Mount Ishizuchi.
Casting its shadow on the mountain top,
A rat flies off.

At the back of the sun,
Where rats pound rice into cakes,
There's a cavity like a mortar pit.

A flyer faster than an airplane,
That's the sparrow.
Mount Ishizuchi, too, flies at a devilish speed,
Ten billion miles a second,
From everlasting to everlasting.

Yet, because there's no time,
And always the same dusk,
It doesn't fly at all:
The peak of Mount Ishizuchi
Has straightened the spine
Of the Island of Futana.

Because there's no space
The airplane doesn't move an inch:
The sun, the plane boarded by the rat,
Are afloat in the sparrow's dream.

That was the best moment of the monk's life.
Firm on a pile of firewood
With nothing more to say, hear, see,
Smoke wrapped him, his folded hands blazed.

There was nothing more to do, the end
Of everything. He remembered, as a cool breeze
Streamed through him, that one is always
In the same place, and that there is no time.

Suddenly a whirling mushroom cloud rose
Before his singed eyes, and he was a mass
Of flame. Globes, one after another, rolled out,
The delighted sparrows flew round like fire balls.

A ship sailed from the back of Nehru's head.
From this alley one has a rather good view
Of the Himalayas, the white undulating peaks
Pressed upon the rotting tilted eaves.

In Goa do the pebbles have eyes?
Nehru's eyes: holes like those in coals
And dry sardines. At dusk his lean shanks
And white Gandhi cap enter an alley.

A streetcar runs along his lashes,
Smoke continues to rise from his body.
At the quaking of the Himalayas,
Mount Everest became a heap of coals.

STRAWBERRY

Like a flower she opens at my side,
Always. Imagine, once
She'd hand me a bowl of milk.

By observing only what's before me,
I'm everywhere, anytime. The flower's
Wax perhaps, phoney as the rest.

Things rising from the mind
Have no real being. What's real
Is the strawberry. And yet.

And yet to call it real is to reject
The rest, all of it. Say she lives,
Why then she lives completely alone.

She breaks a bowl, and now
There's something like a stalk
In her fist, smooth, even.

Overjoyed, she may bite the baby's nose.

OX AND SLEET

When an ox, sleet covered my horns
And, like a bird on a TV antenna,
A rock lodged on the tip of my tongue.
Wind swirls the globe, and there's
A Catholic Sister who, in her white wimple,
Resembles an ox's hoof (the universe
Wavers in the nest of the ox's nose).

When a deer, a maple grew from my leg—
Now whether something's there or not,
What difference? A thing lies neither
Sidelong nor lengthwise, after all,
And this woman breathes life into the universe:
In one breath an ox became a deer.

COCK

Where were you?
Under those leaves piled in the corner?
Dirty cock!
Look—your comb is laced with snow.

You spread your useless wings,
Scratch the earth.
Just what are you about,
Under a heavy sky?

I try your thin warm neck,
And you don't attempt
To shake me off—
Yet you're in agony.

Hopeless! Your beak,
Which should be slashing at my arm,
Is still. Do you really mean
To give up without a flap,

Just one flap of those wings?
I stride through a cold
Wind, a stuffed
Bamboo sheath under the arm.

BACK YARD

The sky clears after rain,
Yellow roses glistening in the light.
Crossing two thresholds, the cat moves off.

Your back is overgrown with nandin leaves.
How awkward your gait!
Like a chicken on damp leaves.
Your necktie, made from skin
Of a tropical fighting fish,
Is hardly subdued. Your yolk-colored
Coat will soon be dyed
With blood again, like a cock's crest.

Let your glances pierce
Like a hedgehog's spines,
I reject them. I can't imagine
What would happen if our glances met.

One day I'll pulverize you.
Now you're scratching
In the bamboo roots, famished.
Watch it—I'll toss you down a hole.

With your cockspurs you kick off
Mars, earth, mankind,
All manner of things, then
Pick over them with your teeth.

Atomic horses bulge through
The pores of a peach-like girl.
The persimmon's leaves are gone again.

THE PIPE

While I slept it was all over,
Everything. My eyes, squashed white,
Flowed off toward dawn.

There was a noise,
Which, like all else, spread and disappeared:
There's nothing worth seeing, listening for.

When I woke, everything seemed cut off.
I was a pipe, still smoking,
Which daylight would knock empty once again.

CROW

The crow, spreading wide wings,
Flapped lazily off.
Soon her young will be doing the same,
Firm wings rustling.

It's hard to tell the male
Crow from the female,
But their love, their mating
Must be fresh as their flight.

Asleep in a night train,
I felt my hat fly off.
The crow was lost in mist,
The engine ploughed into the sea.

WHITE FLOWER

One flower, my family and I,
And I but a petal.
I grasp a hoe in one hand,
Wife and child by the other.

It wasn't I who drove that stake
Into the earth, then pulled it out.
I'm innocent—rather we are,
Like that white cloud above.

I stretch out my right hand: nothing.
I raise my left: nobody.
A white flower opens,
And now I stand apart

While, above, a bomber soars.
My family and I are buried alive.
I'm a handful of earth.
Untraceable.

A SPRAY OF HOT AIR

Trees everywhere, and buds
About to burst in sunlight,
Which makes a river of the snow.

A mongrel rushes up
To the woman pulling
Water from the field well.

It moves rapidly around her
Like a spray of hot air.
Bit by bit she clouds up.

Then, as the mongrel
Leaps about in mist,
She disappears.

CITY

At every breath I'm happier.
What's this? Am I mad again?
I went mad once, then again.

At every breath I'm happier.
I sneeze: an explosion of ash, puff!
The city blazes, disappears.

Once again I'll build myself
A house, fire-proof, pleasant.
I begin carting bricks, with others.

The cornerstone is laid, my dream
Indestructible. But then I sneeze—
The city rises like the phoenix.

MURMURING OF THE WATER

One morning I woke onto a hill
Of withered grasses,
Myself, my family among them.

We swayed, all of us, under the wind,
And so did our shadows.

No more did the laughter of women
Assault my ears,
And I heard the murmuring
Of the limpid water of the Galaxy.

When, desperate, I stretched out
My thin dry arms,
Stars broke from the sky.

PIGEON

The pigeon sleeps with half-closed eyes.
Opened, they fill with azaleas
And space expands before them.
There are white plum blossoms like little faces,
A milky fog about the sun.
The pigeon's no solid, not one or two.

Curiously the red camellia has both stamen, pistil,
And in the mother's dim shrunken bosom a million
    babies,
Hair tips glistening, green necks glittering,
Are like pigeons taking wing.

Yet those eyes are sightless, turned in,
And the bed sheets are like ink stains,
Blurred with babies,
To be wiped clean by the mother's numberless wings.

Now is the time of hydrangeas,
And yellow butterflies flit into the mother's mind,
While the gray pigeons, flying helter skelter,
Cannot escape, drop onto the shoulder of the atomic
    furnace
(They enjoy the faint warmth, bulging like a dream).
On the wire netting, the droppings of nuclear weapons:
Snow falls on my shoulders, a pigeon sails off alone.

MUMMY

Resuscitated
By the kiss of a bat
On its papyrus mouth
And the Nile's spring thrust,
The mummy arose amidst
The jolting pillars
And strode from the cave,
Followed by a throng of bats.

Tripping on a pyramid step,
The mummy was landed upon
By a bat, a sarcophagus lid,
Who, by patting its head with her wing,
Unwound the mummy's cloth,
Dipped it in the Nile,
Then wrapped it round herself
From claw-tips to shoulders.
She lay down—a mummy.

Tail up, the sphinx came
To sniff her all over,
But the bat was fast asleep.
How many centuries have slipped by?
The dam's dried up,
This once submerged temple
Stands again,
Its stone birds
Have once more taken flight.

RED WAVES

A cat, a black-white tabby out of nowhere,
Licks its back at the water's edge:
Perhaps—with that bit of metal dangling
From her middle—a space cat,
Readying to fly off again.

But how to ask her? I opened my hand, wide,
Just in front of her face, at which
She flipped over, legs up and pointing
Toward the sea in the pose of a 'beckoning cat'.

The sea obliged: she was carried off
Bobbing on the waves. Was she drowned?
I asked myself over and over,
Alone for hours on the moonlit beach.

Suddenly a red parasol came rolling
Toward me—the cat's? It danced along
The windless shore, with me chasing full tilt.
I didn't have a chance. Come daybreak
I spotted the parasol rising above a rock:
The sun, blinding! Red waves reached my ankles.

SPARROW IN WINTER

Breastdown fluttering in the breeze,
The sparrow's full of air holes.
Let the winds of winter blow,
Let them crack a wing, two,
The sparrow doesn't care.

The air streams through him, free, easy,
Scattering feathers, bending legs.
He hops calmly, from branch to empty branch
In an absolutely spaceless world.

I'd catch, skewer, broil you,
But my every shot misses: you're impossible.
All at once there's the sound
Of breaking glass, and houses begin
To crumple. Rising quickly,
An atomic submarine nudges past your belly.

THE MARTIAN ROCK

The Thames beneath my hands,
The Seine underfoot: I'm always alone,
Trampling your heads,
You who are as so many watermelon pips.

You are so many, clinging
To my arms, thighs:
I split you on the tip of my tongue.
The Sumida River stinks
(There's nothing between us),
Mine is the Tone River's mouth
(You breathe no longer, dead).

Hard rain across the earth,
And through the mist
A red headlight.
The wind flows through me,
Toes to ears:
I'm gassified to nothingness.

What use have eyes?
I'm somewhere, nowhere.
High in the air a hand beckons,
And I'm off again, flying.

When I come down
The Martian rock will split.

DESTRUCTION

The universe is forever falling apart—
No need to push the button,
It collapses at a finger's touch:
Why, it barely hangs on the tail of a sparrow's eye.

The universe is so much eye secretion,
Hordes leap from the tips
Of your nostril hairs. Lift your right hand:
It's in your palm. There's room enough
On the sparrow's eyelash for the whole.

A paltry thing, the universe:
Here is all strength, here the greatest strength.
You and the sparrow are one
And, should he wish, he can crush you.
The universe trembles before him.

DISCLOSURE

The sparrow sleeps, thinking of nothing.
Meanwhile the universe has shrunk to half.
He's attached by a navel string, swimming
In a sea of fluid, amniotic, slightly bitter.

The centre is 'severance'—no sound at all—
Until the navel string is snapped. All of which
Was told by her as she sat astride Pegasus,
The poet on a circuit of the universe.

The sparrow came at her, bill like a sword,
And suddenly from her buttocks—the sun!
The sparrow carried the stained sheets
To the moon. On drawing the clouds apart,

He discovered the cold corpse of Mars.
Not once had he disclosed the secrets of his life.

THE HARE

The hare was in the misty rubbish,
Ruby eyed, knowing no hindrance.
The tide laps the soul's shore,
There are shoals beyond the stars.

A blue tree blossomed there,
A wall heavy with ivy.
Sea and mountains, like dust specks,
Were floating in the soul.

The hare leapt, danced above the rubbish—
Soul's the one reality,
Nothing extending beyond it.
So roared the sea in the hare's head.

DUCK

The duck stood on the mountain top,
Then, spreading wings, leapt down

To where the sea was chanting, chanting,
White ripples moving up the beach.

Again the duck went up the mountain path,
Overgrown with summer grasses,

And waddled through the cedars, watery
Cool, dark except where sunlight caught

Green leaves. Try as she might,
The duck could not regain the mountain top.

Summer passed, and it was spring again.
I wrenched off my silver watch

And tossed it in a rosebed: yellow
Petals fell like feathers on the duckbill.

WHAT IS MOVING

When I turned to look back
Over the waters
The sky was birdless.

Men *were, are* born.
Do I still live? I ask myself,
Munching a sweet potato.

Don't smell of death,
Don't cast its shadow.
Any woman when I glance her way,
Looks down,
Unable to stand it.
Men, as if dead,
Turn up the whites of their eyes.

Get rid of those trashy ideas—
The same thing
Runs through both of us.
My thought moves the world:
I move, it moves.
I crook my arm, the world's crooked.

AUTUMN FLOWERS

Exactly thirty years ago my father died,
While autumn flowers were fading.
What's happened since? Don't ask him—
He probably doesn't even know I live!

Father, now as old as you at death,
I'm weary. Yet one must go on, beyond time,
Which in any case does not exist.
Pigeons shoot up, millions of them

Nest in my little toes. I must live
Beyond the smoke and clouds, as all else
Without dimension, succession, relationship.
Await the fading of the flowers.

THE PEACH

A little girl under a peach tree,
Whose blossoms fall into the entrails
Of the earth.

There you stand, but a mountain may be there
Instead; it is not unlikely that the earth
May be yourself.

You step against a plate of iron and half
Your face is turned to iron. I will smash
Flesh and bone

And suck the cracked peach. She went up the mountain
To hide her breasts in the snowy ravine.
Women's legs

Are more or less alike. The leaves of the peach tree
Stretch across the sea to the end of
The continent.

The sea was at the little girl's beck and call.
I will cross the sea like a hairy
Caterpillar

And catch the odour of your body.

ONE HUNDRED BILLIONTH OF A SECOND

How long will this happiness last?
Why, not one hundred billionth of a second—
Appalling! If I permit myself to think,
The farther I'll be from the truth.

To think, muse, is to substitute time,
That beggar's dirty bag, for truth,
Which lasts one hundred billionth of a second.
Time isn't, nor space. 'Thinking over',

Sheer impossibility. Isn't happiness
To reside there in peace?
No, 'to reside there in peace' is misleading,
Since *there* nothing of time exists.

There's no continuous subjective being,
No place for correlation.
Happiness—a mere bit of sentimentality,
Which neither lasts nor fades.

QUAILS

It is the grass that moves, not the quails.
Weary of embraces, she thought of
Committing her body to the flame.

When I shut my eyes, I hear far and wide
The air of the Ice Age stirring.
When I open them, a rocket passes over a meteor.

A quail's egg is complete in itself,
Leaving not room enough for a dagger's point.
All the phenomena in the universe: myself.

Quails are supported by the universe
(I wonder if that means subsisting by God).
A quail has seized God by the neck

With its black bill, because there is no
God greater than a quail.
(Peter, Christ, Judas: a quail.)

A quail's egg: idle philosophy in solution.
(There is no wife better than a quail.)
I dropped a quail's egg into a cup for buckwheat
    noodles,

And made havoc of the Democratic Constitution.
Split chopsticks stuck in the back, a quail husband
Will deliver dishes on a bicycle, anywhere.

The light yellow legs go up the hill of Golgotha.
Those quails who stood on the rock, became the rock!
The nightfall is quiet, but inside the congealed exuviae

Numberless insects zigzag, on parade.

FLOWER

I'm a billion removes
From myself: the fire,
Though red, is cold.

I'm a steel-petalled
Flower, root and all.
Though white, the water's solid.

I'm burnt out, corroded,
And yet transparent.
My woman's like an orange.

STILLNESS

A cock crows and someone
Strums a *koto*.
Nothing's wanting.

In the midst of this stillness,
I'm still.
Could I catch it, I'd drop

That butterfly into my mouth.

HORSE

Young girls bloom like flowers.
Unharnessed, a horse trots
Round its driver who
Grasps it by a rope.

Far off a horse is going round and round
In a square plot.

Not miserable, not cheerful either,
The bay horse is prancing,
Shaking its head, throwing up its legs
By turn: it is not running.

But there are no spectators
In what looks like an amphitheater.

White cherry petals fall like snowflakes
In the wind. All at once,
Houses, people vanish, into silence.
Nothing moves. Streetcars, buses, are held back
Silently. Quiet, everything.
All visible things become this nothingness.

The horse's bones—beautiful in their gray sheen.

A horse is going round and round,
Dancing now, with *joie de vivre*,
Under the cliff of death.

MISTY RAIN

A misty rain falls this morning,
A phantom dog creeps along.

As I sit drinking a cup of tea
An amorphous cat leaps on my lap.

For awhile in my imaginary tea garden
I arrange rocks and plant bamboos.

Then, with the fall of cloud-swept night,
I close the window and turn in.

COLLAPSE

Time oozed from my pores,
Drinking tea
I tasted the seven seas.

I saw in the mist formed
Around me
The fatal chrysanthemum, myself.

Its scent choked, and as I
Rose, squaring
My shoulders, the earth collapsed.

SUN

Stretched in the genial sun
The mountain snake
Tickled its length along the rock.

The wind rustled the sunshine,
But the snake,
Fully uncoiled, was calm.

Fifty thousand years ago!
Later the same sun
Blazed across the pyramids,

Now it warms my chest.
But below, through
Shattered rock, the snake

Thrusts up its snout, fangs
Flicking at my thoughts
Strewn about the rocks like violets.

It's you, faces cut like triangles,
Have kept the snake alive!
The pavement's greened with leaves.

WORDS

I don't take your words
Merely as words.
Far from it.

I listen
To what makes you talk—
Whatever that is—
And me listen.

RAIN

The rain keeps falling,
Even in dreams.
The skull leaks badly.

There's a constant dripping
Down the back.
The rain, which no one

Remembers starting,
Keeps falling,
Even on the finest days.

CHIDORI POOL

When I was sailing on the Chidori Pool
Of the outer moat,
There was the fragrance of cherry blossoms.

Somewhere cherries are in flower,
Or they may not be—
Who cares?

A sweet-sour fragrance quickly fading,
Coming from where?
The Cemetery of Unknown Soldiers?

BREAM

What's land? What's water?
In the window of the florist
Swims the big-eyed bream,
Between dahlias, chrysanthemums.

So you're alone? Well, forget
Others, keep talking to yourself.
Past the hydrangea leaves
Sways the scaly bream-mass.

History? Look between
The dry leaves of the sardine
Paper. Oops! the anemone's
Finally snagged a scale,

And flowering on a tulip stem,
The bream's tail and fin!
Why fear? What do you know
Of what happens after death?

Just remember to pierce
The cactus through your Christmas hat.
Brushed by trumpet lilies, roses,
The bream opens/shuts his mouth.

TIME

Before I knew it I was on a beach,
Legs wet. I'm not sure when,
But I was there near the hydrangeas,
Under a darkening sky. Then as the salt
Dried on my legs the sea flashed, sunlit.

I'm not sure where I was, perhaps
On the shore of the sea of memory.
Still, I was there, and am there now:
Overwhelming the bright/dark of reality.

CAT

A quiet, a very quiet place
With camellias in bloom.

Their redness faded, nothing
Else remained. The image

Itself vanished—it might
Have been the white magnolias.

A gray cat squats there,
Pale blue earth between its paws.

THE POSITION OF THE SPARROW

The sparrow has cut the day in half:
Afternoons—yesterday's, the day after tomorrow's—
Layer the white wall.
Those of last year, and next year's too,
Are dyed into the wall—see them?—
And should the wall come down,
Why, those afternoons will remain,
Glimmering, just as they are, through time.
(That was a colourless realm where,
Nevertheless, most any colour could well up.)

Just as the swan becomes a crow,
So everything improves—everything:
No evil *can* persist, and as to things,
Why, nothing is unchangeable.
The squirrel, for instance, is on the tray,
Buffalos lumber through African brush,
The snail wends along the wall,
Leaving a silver trail.
The sparrow's bill grips a pomegranate seed:
Just anything can resemble a lens, or a squirrel.

Because the whole is part, there's not a whole,
Anywhere, that is not part.
And all those happenings a billion years ago,
Are happening now, all around us: time.
Indeed this morning the sparrow hopped about
In that nebulous whirlpool
A million light years hence.

And since the morning is void,
Anything can be. Since mornings
A billion years from now are nothingness,
We can behold them.
The sparrow stirs,
The universe moves slightly.

LIFE INFINITE

Beyond words, this no-thingness within,
Which I've become. So to remain

Only one thing's needed: Zen sitting.
I think, breathe with my whole body—

Marvellous. The joy's so pure,
It's beyond love making, anything.

I can see, live anywhere, everywhere.
I need nothing, not even life.

PAPER DOOR

The shoji blocks the winter sun.
As fallen leaves shift, scattering,
So goes history: the eye and its subject fused.

The eyes, turned sardines, are broiling
On the grill. The torn shoji flaps in the wind.
Like the universe, its frames are fading.

The drinker is silhouetted on the shoji,
And there's tea's subtle odour:
Tea whisked, like cares, into a froth.

DECK

If time is but a stream flowing from past to future,
Why, it's nothing more than sardine guts!
If all is carried away by it,
Then everything is seaweed along a desolate strand!
Has this stream no end at all?
Then there ought to be an unmapped sea around it.

The tide moves at its own sweet will,
Yet whether it moves or not—who cares?
Still, an absolutely immobile ship is by the quay:
Should its anchor drop to the depths of time,
We'll have had it, the harbor will dry up.

A sailor goes ashore, walking along
With existence in the palm of his hand.
With nothing under him,
His tapering toes extend,
Then—like a meteor—disappear.

The sailor is free to go anywhere,
No deck is bigger than his hand.

SPRING SNOW

A flurry of flakes—
Flame, smoke, humankind—,
Wild flakes like an insect cloud,
Bombers saturating.

This globe, like a lump
Of snow gripped in the fist.
Now one can't see through it,
The firm flakes binding.

THE CLOUD AND THE
BUTTERFLY

The idea that's just popped into my head
Is that butterfly settled
On the field's warped bamboo fence.

At times it just gathers wings and rests,
Then flits wildly about the field:
The fence has nothing to do with the butterfly,
I have nothing to do with my idea.

Go dig in the field, you won't find me:
I'm neither field nor fence.

There's a white cloud above,
But I'm not that either.
The cloud? It seeks the butterfly
Which, wings folded, lies on the cold ground.

ON A DAY OF CONTINUOUS RAIN

On a day of continuous rain
I sliced my finger.
White as the distant past,
The rain would not cease.

My finger, like a witch's red eye,
Kept on bleeding.
The future drips from a finger end:
Avoid the smell of blood.

BLACK SMOKE

I have thrown my 'me' away:
The river willows bud pale blue.

Where did I toss that 'me'?
I sought it in wind and water.

Resigned, I looked up:
A cat at the controls of a helicopter!

Landing and sidling up to me,
Where I lay flat on my back, she asked:

'Have you emerged from the earth—you?'
'Who—me?'

'Well then, what's that grass sprouting
All over your behind?'

Out shot my hand and grabbed
The cat's tail, which I was still holding
When the helicopter went up again.

At last I had found my 'me',
I thought, but not for long.

Night fell silently, but high above
Two glittering eyeballs wouldn't disappear.

They were burning on me,
As if the 'me' I'd abandoned,
Overpowered by loneliness,
Was frantically craving me.

Oh, I understood that those eyeballs
Might have been the cat's—
How she must have suffered without her tail!

I lit a cigarette, black smoke rose,
Then I quickly buried it.

Then came a most marvellous idea:
Even if I didn't find my 'me',
I'd still have my tail!

EVENING CLOUDS

Something like cloud is spread over the sky,
The earth, too, is something like cloud.

Fingers stripped of their gold foil,
Overspread the earth, black as cloud shadows.

At sunset, when clouds burst into flame,
The fingers move.

MASCOT

Somebody is breathing inside me—
Birds, the very earth.

The ocean's in my chest. Walking,
I always throw myself down.

Newssheets, a puppy were dancing in the wind—
Trucks rushed by,

Empty trucks stout enough to carry the earth
On their puncture-proof tires.

The instant I raised my hand to wave,
I was nowhere.

The puppy was sprawled out on its belly,
Run over—again, again.

You're a badger, I'll bet, posing as a mascot
With that moonlit tie

And, sticking from your pocket, night's flower.

WIND

Give it words,
Stick limbs on it,
You won't alter essence.
Whereas the wind—

I'll live gently
As the wind, flying
Over the town,
My chest full of sparrows.

WIND AMONG THE PINES

The wind blows hard among the pines
Toward the beginning
Of an endless past.
Listen: you've heard everything.

STITCHES

My wife is always knitting, knitting:
Not that I watch her,
Not that I know what she thinks.

(Awake till dawn
I drowned in your eyes—
I must be dead:
Perhaps it's the mind that stirs.)

With that bamboo needle
She knits all space, piece by piece,
Hastily hauling time in.

Brass-cold, exhausted,
She drops into bed and,
Breathing calmly, falls asleep.

Her dream must be deepening,
Her knitting coming loose.

SUN AND FLOWERS

Though I can't decide whether
There are three suns or ten moons,
I lack for nothing,
Here, sprawled on the grass:
When hungry, I'll eat anything.

COMET

A word swims through the air—
Fish; vomited dust speck;
Jet through the sound barrier,
Full of Thames fog.
How far is it flying?

A man wrings out a casting net
In the upper reaches of the Milky Way:
Rain pours through his brains,
Cliffs reveal themselves.

The sun, ah the sun, is dissolved
In blue, and now seer and seen
Are one: wet, smoky.

There were no rocks around,
The word plunged down the precipice—
Now blanched, dead,
Mere time carcass, it sways
Like seaweed on the beach.

Its eyes devoured by crows,
The waves splash over it.

Then as from inside a violoncello
Someone said to himself:
'The sun is hidden
In a single sand grain'.

An airfield too luxuriant with word endings,
Contact of white and black clouds
Followed by thunder—
The birth of new figures.

The moment it is announced
It rises with the globe
Into the stratosphere,
Up to the shores of constellations,
The word.

IMMUTABILITY

Immutable: no need of eyes and ears
Which, in any case, are no more use
Than glass beads and bamboo tubes.
Nothing can be done about me, who am nothing.

SNAIL

The snail crawls over blackness.

Just now, in the garden,
A solid lump of snow
Slipped from the zinc roof
To behead the nandin.

Make it snappy!

In full view a stalk has been
Torn off:
Let the wind rage over the earth,
He is unaware.

His head flies to the end
Of the world,
His body is tossed
Into the ash can.

Could it be that he's the falling snow?

HERE

This hut is larger than the earth,
Since there's nothing that is not.
In the small charcoal stove

Burn sun and countless stars,
And the corners of the kitchen
Buzz with humankind.

IF I AM FLOWERS

Flowers blossom on my back,
Fall withered across my thighs.
Yet though they bloom all over me,
I can't see them.
Try as I might—and I do—
I can't be anything but flowers.
How clean and bright!

I don't look at a man and think: man.
Nor, for that matter,
Do I think him ox or pig.
He is I. And as meaningless.

STATUE OF KUDARA-AVALOKITESVARA

She holds a frail jar in her hand
Into which she has poured nothing,
No life's joy or giddying brew—
Only a billion worlds!

FISH

I hold a newspaper, reading.
Suddenly my hands become cow ears,
Then turn into Pusan, the South Korean port.

Lying on a mat
Spread on the bankside stones,
I fell asleep.
But a willow leaf, breeze-stirred,
Brushed my ear.
I remained just as I was,
Near the murmurous water.

When young there was a girl
Who became a fish for me.
Whenever I wanted fish
Broiled in salt, I'd summon her.
She'd get down on her stomach
To be sun-cooked on the stones.
And she was always ready!

Alas, she no longer comes to me.
An old benighted drake,
I hobble homeward.
But look, my drake feet become horse hoofs!
Now they drop off
And, stretching marvellously,
Become the tracks of the Tokaido Railway Line.

COCK

Getting soaked on rainy days,
Tramping snow on snowy,
Riding wind on windy days,
Strutting on the fine—
I'll crow a lifetime through.

CRAB

The crab polished
Its claws
In the shade of a tree.

Suddenly a wave
Baring white teeth
Swallowed crab and shade.

The crab,
Sunk to the bed of the sea,
Forgot the sunlit sand.

ANTS

Nothing exists, yet fascinating
The ants scurrying in moonlight.

It is the eye deceives:
The ants—they are but moonlight.

The idea of being's impossible:
There's neither moon nor ants.

SUN

It's a fine day
And I'm talking with the sun.
'I don't think there's only one sun,'

I say. 'There are no end of you,
And of course there are the stars:
To be means to be numberless.

And yet, O magnificent,
I delight in your heat.
Dust speck, I adore you.'

SUN THROUGH THE LEAVES

The babe's asleep on the mother's back.
No good your turning to the plum tree—
The scent of blossoms is perilous.
The tree may really be the blue sea,
Yet the sound of waves cannot reach
The stone of a pickled plum, nor wake the babe.

This body, its leaping heart, tumbles,
Hurls itself into the sea. Root up the trees!
Daily the babe kicks up the heavens,
Kicks down the earth. At will—right now—
The universe can be destroyed easily as a dog.
Sunbeams, spokes of a stopped wheel,
Blaze through the leaves of a branch.

MAGPIE

I start across the bridge.
Coming toward me from the other side,
A woman, drenched and perhaps
Having failed to purchase apples, mutters—
'Sardines, sardines'. Below, listening,
A magpie bobs mournfully up and down.

It is a long black bridge,
So long that to cross it is unthinkable.
My white breath dies, rises and dies.
Life: dust on a bridge rail.
Wars, revolutions: bubbles on a stream.

Late in the frosty night, alone,
I cross an endless bridge.

A RICHER GROUND

The bus roars through cherry blossoms
Or a snowstorm. Who knows?

I'm not on it, but then again
I'm not not on it. Who knows?

Seals glide across an iceberg,
Where bound? Who knows?

Of course I may be quite wrong,
Which in any case is unavoidable.

The question 'To be or not to be'
Just isn't fair. I stand on richer ground.

PENGUINS

Penguins waddle across the Antarctic
Without hands, shadows.
There's no life, no death,
Stopping, advancing,
Raining, blossoming.

I had a fish drying in the sun
To eat. Well, there was
Neither fish nor sun.
Penguins do not eat, and all night through
The sun roams the bottom of the sea.

IVIES

Smoke from my pipe
Circled the earth,
Entering the sky of England.

In London a concrete library
Is smothered with ivies.
A rat peered from a window,
Then a woman with glasses
Drew the curtains, the end of her story.
The ivies shone crimson in the setting sun.

I might have seen all this on television,
But there is no need. My eyes, though closed,
Are clear, even when squinty from pipe smoke:
In that smoke move sun, moon, stars.

Now there are factory chimneys
Around the woman's head,
Workers rushing about on the tips
Of her nostril hairs. There's the strong
Smell of cigar in the Thames fog
Which has drifted over Tokyo.

SPARROW

The sparrow, while shaving,
Cuts off his head,
Which is precisely what he wants.
Thin hairs float in the pond.

The sparrow has no fear of death,
Is indifferent to the grass
Sprouting on the roof, the footsteps
Below. Yet he leaps mightily

In that dream which spreads
His wings like the eagle's.
Really what pleases most
Is that he may survive the rape blossoms.

The sparrow's head is empty,
Marvellously. And once dead
There'll be no further need
To chatter chatter, and twist

His head about. The sparrow
Struggles at the noble task
Of mixing time, makes a mess
Of something he'd have ended.

APRICOT

There's a deep inlet in the upper region of her body,
Apricots are ripe in the village on the bay.
The temple bell is sunk firm on the lake bed
And overhead a crow oars through the rain.

In spring there are red flowers,
And the bluest fish move through blue water—
A sign of pregnancy. Now sleet falls
Upon her shoulders and the windows rattle.

Heaven and earth split wide: birth—
A sheep with no horns. Is it a pram
That cloud wheels above? Smell of stained blanket
From the atom reactor. What's a pacifist to do?

WHITE PAPER

I was walking on white paper.
However far I went, there
I remained, between the print,
Making no attempt to read, of course,
Part of the paper itself.

She was correcting proofs
With red ink. At a puff of wind
The paper stirred, and I saw
That she badly needed
A haircut. Miserable.

'I'll bring you fame!' I cried,
Then continued to walk
Until, before me, I saw a book,
Unopened. A fossil. I stepped
Over it and, without a glance, moved on.

ON THE WIND

I was walking on the wind,
Below me Mount Fuji
And the sea, size of a stamp,
Islands like so many ants.

I slapped the sun with my right hand,
Held the moon in my left,
Not once forgetting that unborn
I had been a cloud.

I dashed through time, the future
Small as a needle's eye
Through which I passed like thread,
Body hunched, an immovable tininess.

LIKE DEWDROPS

The earth broke into pieces—
Like dewdrops, like beads.

Sitting to one side, umbrella
In hand, as if about to voyage,

The devil told innumerable
Lies. Mankind, dead and gone,

Existed in some legend. Stars
Pattered—hailstones, rocks.

Suddenly, unmasked at last, God—
Devil that he was—disintegrated

Into the shadows of the earth,
Like the engine of a crashed plane.

APEX OF THE UNIVERSE

Standing with cold bare feet
Atop the universe,
Raking down the ashes of logic,
My voice will be fresh again.

I've had more than enough
Of the polite sexuality of wind
And stars. It's not science that beats
The black into the parrot's bill.

Without hands and little spirit,
I'll blow and blow
Till that fresh sound comes:
I refuse to hear of the fate of wingless birds.

ICE

Lately I sat on the ice and spat clouds about—
To whom shall I speak of the delight
Of being transformed into a weird little spirit?

There I was, merging with all those colours
Which, after swimming between Mars and Saturn,
Passed the other side of the frosted glass.

It may be called, to be sure, the minute will
Of the rain and be smoke-warm. O this drive
Toward self-repletion, self-extinction!

(Strange, this sudden relief
When I jerk from my lip the fish hook
Lodged there when I ripped the head of an eel.)

Some may call it deception, evasion,
Others scorn it as the moralist's porcelain nobility—
Yet, O pure-hearted one, slash the soft skin

Of idea with a knife that can rend a wall. Don't count
On the exquisite calculation of disrupted feelings.
O wind full of carnal odours, slap feet to ears!

Then, burning at once that mop of wild hair,
Face yourself as for the first time:
Cherish the distance from joy found in its denial.

WHAT DASHES?

The fat white cat lies beneath
The ginger leaves. I'm closer, closer,
And will nab him yet. The rain
Comes down hard, and the load
On my back's sky-high. When I've
Skinned him, ah, I'll boil him with ginger.

The plectrum with which I strum
My *samisen's* alive with rhythms,
And I draw ever nearer to the future
Which is wrapped in twilit shadow.
Escape's impossible, and how tiresome
The god of science and mathematics!

His face resembles that of the cat
Which drowned in the Nile. Precisely!
The cat of Nabeshima, with those big
Sun-like eyes, no longer laps
The obscene oil where he awaits
Morning as if nothing has happened.

Stand free and easy under reality's
Blue sky, brush aside the cobwebbed
Past and pierce the sooty roof. Now!
A figtree's chopped down, and suddenly
The cat has disappeared. What dashes?
Nothing.

WILD CAMOMILES

I was at the foot of a department store
Escalator when I died. I was walking
A prehistoric pavement, remembering ancestors.

On the plane I gave the stewardess
A folding screen on which was painted
The slope where I, an enormous rock upturned,
Was born. Mountains became rivers, cars, reptiles.

In the basement of the department store
I bought a dried mackerel-earth, a mushroom-sun,
Knowing it might have been my last chance
To comfort her on the trip. Soon
The plane landed near the entrance to a cave
Where shamelessly I flirted with an ancient beauty.
All about there were wild camomiles, small, faded.

It was then, remembering my love
For the stewardess, I rushed back to the plane.

THE SOLID SEASON

A pinetree's rooted in the flowerpot,
And the room smells of an Adonis.

I go out for a swim and though a bit
Too swift the tide's sweet as an orange.

I lie down naked by the daffodils,
Summer settling ahead of me in the wine cup.

Melting rock salt with my body heat,
I eat the solid season made of myself.

Help yourself, please. Whether hot or cold,
This laver's lighter than the soul.

LOVEBIRD

What's living—fission of mother and child?
Snake with tail in its fangs?
Fusion/dispersion of tortoise-shaped carbon?

The lovebird flew her coop,
Breastdown and quick brown wings
Expanding/contracting in the cold air,
Her joy, like a rainbow, describing a semi-circle.

The lovebird tries to brush off light,
But her face is already decomposed,
Legs frozen.

Her ideal: to be beautifully dead,
Like an Italian sculpture. Death may give
Her as many legs as a head has hairs,
Trees may grow forest thick from her body.

The lovebird died miserably,
Hanging there like an icicle,
And now an empty cage
Spans the concrete windowsill.

To transform all this into one tile
And slap it on some roof—
Is that living?

RAT AND WOMAN

What's master of the body?
Not mind or spirit.
It's somewhere in the mind's depths,
Pervading the universe.

To herd a flock of sheep
Is beyond the power of dogs.
No, it's the shepherd—God?—
Swinging a rat's tail.

There's snow on the ground
And, on the hillock, a naked woman.
Now I'm free to do anything
On sure ground.

Nothing gives offence:
My every deed,
Free as the mind itself,
Leaves not a trace.

BODY

My body's been torn to pieces,
Limbs sway in the wind
Like those of the persimmon,
Thick with blue leaves.

Suddenly a butterfly,
My eyeballs spots
On its wings,
Takes off, brilliant.

Future's circled by a crumbling
Earthen wall, and the dog's
Pregnant with earth,
Nipples of its swollen teats

Sharp as lead in a red pencil.
As I rushed through flame
An airplane passed between
My legs. Sky's my body.

AFTERIMAGES

The volcanic smoke of Mount Aso
Drifted across the sea, white ash
Clinging to mulberry leaves
And crowning the heads of sparrows.

An open-mouthed lava crocodile;
A sparrow like a fossil sprig,
The moon filling its eyes;
A colossal water lizard stuck to a dead tree,
Its headland tail quaking.

A cloud floats in my head—beautiful!
When the sparrow opens its eyes,
Nothing but rosy space. All else gone.

Don't tell me that tree was red—
The only thing that moved, ever closer,
Was a girl's nose. All mere afterimages.

Water, coldness itself, flows underfoot.

The sparrow, eyes half closed, lay in an urn
In the pit. Now it fans up. The earth's
Fiery column is nearly extinguished.